I CAN MAKE MY OWN PRAYERS

I CAN MAKE MY OWN PRAYERS

LUCILLE E. HEIN
Illustrated by Joan Orfe

JUDSON PRESS, Valley Forge

I CAN MAKE MY OWN PRAYERS

Judson Press, Valley Forge, Pa. 19481

International Standard Book No. 0-8170-0528-5
Library of Congress Catalog Card No. 72-154026

Printed in the U.S.A.

To mothers and fathers
who have taught their children
to talk with God

To You Who Use This Book with a Child

A young child learns his prayers from adults. Sometimes he learns only formal prayers, that is, words and concepts that are often beyond his understanding. But he needs other prayers, too, informal and spontaneous prayers.

A child who is being brought up in the love of God often talks with God in his own way. His approach is conversational. He talks to God as to a friend.

Listen for a child's creative, imaginative, spontaneous, and personal approach to God. Help your child to use his conversations with God as prayers.

Read the next page, "I Can Make My Own Prayers," to your child. Then read one of the episodes to him. He will be interested in the child in the book who makes his own prayers.

Talk with your child about God and prayer. Tell him he can talk with God any time, any place, for any reason, about anything. Suggest that he make his own prayer for a particular time, perhaps when he goes to bed or when he is very happy. Help him to find words that rhyme. He cannot yet write, but you can write his words on paper. He will find his prayer easy to remember because it is his very own prayer. He made it.

I Can Make My Own Prayers

I can make a prayer
all my own.
Mother says
I need not wait
till I am grown.
She says
I do not need
big words.
After all,
she says,
God hears
birds.

Dear God
Help me make a prayer
all my own, to use when you
and I talk alone.
Amen.

Dear God
Here I am,
looking for you.
Maybe you
are looking, too?

If I am quiet,
will I hear God speak?
Will God hear me?

I can be quiet—

as quiet as a bud
opening to be a flower

as quiet as a snowflake
falling on a snowdrift

as quiet as a bug
skating on the water

as quiet as a cat
padding by

as quiet as a worm
exploring in the rain

as quiet as a stone
hidden underground

as quiet as a tired bird
sleeping in a tree.

Dear God,
I am quiet
I wait
I listen
I hear.
Thank you, God, for being near.
Amen.

I like to talk with someone
when I play alone.

Sometimes I talk with my tricycle
or my wagon.
Sometimes I talk with my pretend friends.
They are twins,
Nancy and Clancy.
Sometimes I talk with my dog,
Laddie.

Sometimes I talk with God.

Like this.

Here I am, God,
having fun.
Watch me jump!
See me run!

We talk a lot at my house
about God's beautiful world.

I know I must take care
of God's beautiful world
and all God's things.
God's things can be used over and over
if I am careful.

Like dirt.

First I take dirt from the garden,
add water,
make mud pies for lunch,
let them harden.

After I eat,
I tip out the mud pies
and they make dirt again
for the garden.

It is like a circle.

Daddy says everything is part of a circle made by God
and I am a part of that circle.

Dear God,
I will take care
of the world
for it is yours.
Thank you for letting me use your world.
Amen.

Sunday is a different day.

The streets are empty
on Sunday.

I go to Sunday school
and sometimes to church.

I like Sunday school.
My teacher tells a story.
We sing a song.
Sometimes I make a picture.

I have a paper to take home,
and Mother reads it to me.

We have a prayer to say
in Sunday school.
I try to remember it
and say it for Mother and Daddy
when I am home.

I have made my own prayer for Sunday.
This is my prayer.

Dear God,

Your world is big and
your love is bigger.
I like my corner of
your world and my
corner of your love.

Amen.

I think God has fun
decorating the sky.

He hangs out the sun
in the morning.
Sometimes he pastes up a few clouds.

He hangs up the moon
and scatters stars
on the blackness
of night.

God gives me night and day.

How can I thank God for all he gives?

I have made a prayer to thank him.

Dear God,
Thank you for making night and day,
with time for sleep and time for play.
Amen.

I like
when Daddy and I go for a walk
at night.

We walk to the park
at the end of my street
where the houses end.

Everything is different
at night.

There are patches of bright moonlight
and patches that are dark and scary
where the moon does not reach.

Men have walked on the moon.
Maybe I will. Someday.

Being out at night
makes me feel strange and lonely.
I walk close to Daddy.

I hope that you are near me, God,
watching me
in the dark.

Dear God,

Please walk with me
to show the way
and keep me safe
by night and day.

Amen.

When I do too many somersaults,
I see the sun circling and exploding.

When I roll down the grassy hill
in the park,
the clouds roll with me.

When I swing very high,
the trees bend down
to meet me.

When I race my trike,
the wind races me.

When I eat snow,
my insides giggle.

People who know,
like Mother and Daddy,
tell me it is you, God,
who makes
the sun
and clouds
and grassy hills
and trees
and wind
and snow.

Dear God,
I love your world. Thank you
for making it so beautiful
for me.

Amen.

At my house
we like to make our own prayers
for Thanksgiving
and Easter
and New Year's Day
and birthdays of great men.

What I like best
is when we make prayers
for Christmas.

We made a family prayer
to say on Christmas Eve.

Each of us made one part of the prayer,
and Daddy wrote it down.

Our prayer was very long
when he put all the parts together.
But my part was short,
and I said my part first.

Long ago
a baby came
to earth.
Jesus was
his name.
And this is
the night
of his birth.

A day I like is my birthday
or someone else's birthday.

In my family
we have a party for each birthday.
We have it
When Daddy is home to eat with us.

The one whose birthday it is
sits at a special place at the table.
Our presents are around his place.

For dessert we have cake and ice cream.
There are candles on the cake,
and the one whose birthday it is
blows out the candles.
He says his birthday prayer
when he blows out the candles.

This is the prayer I say
when it is my birthday
and I blow out the candles.
I made this prayer myself.

My birthday is a happy day
of fun and gifts and love.
Thank you God, for giving me
my family—and your love.

Do you have your very own birthday prayer?

Sometimes I make my own prayers this way.
I think of things I like—

Then I thank God for them.

Sometimes my thank you's
make a prayer that sounds like a poem.
And I surprise myself.
I am a poet!

Dear God,
Thank you
for trees
and honey bees
for flowers
and puddling showers
for my toy boat
and my new coat
for Mother
and my brother
for my dog, Laddie,
and my walks with Daddy
for the sun
and all my fun.
Amen.

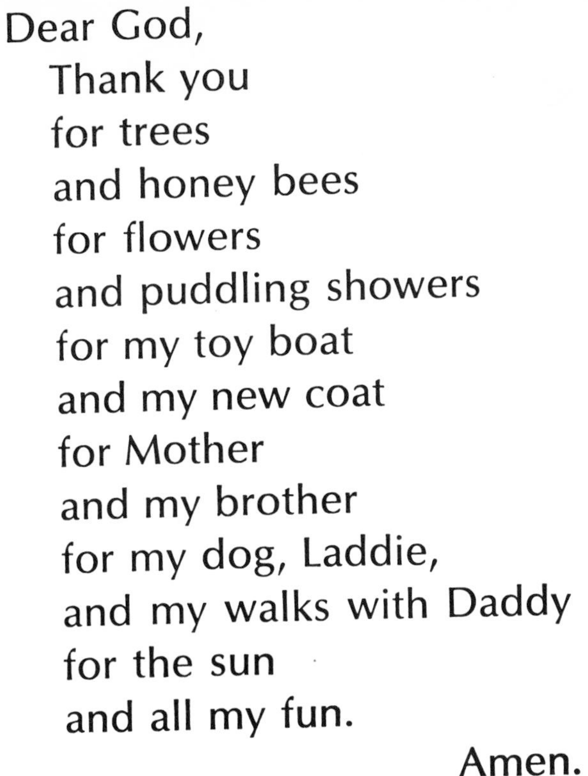

What do you thank God for?
Make a poem about it.

Do you like to go to bed?

I do.

When I am ready for bed,
I feel so soft
and warm
and safe.

And so sleepy that I can hardly say
this prayer I made for bedtime.

Goodnight, God.
I am going to bed.
Thank you for the day I had.
Thank you for the day ahead.
Amen.

I have other bedtime prayers.
Sometimes I say this one.

Dear God,
Please hold me in your love tonight.
Wake me when the world is bright.
Bless everyone who lives with me.
Bless everyone I cannot see.
Amen.

When I am very, very sleepy
I say a very short prayer.

Dear God,
Hold me tight
through the night.
Amen.